A Bigger Band-Aid

Hope for parents abused as children

Ronae Jull

ISBN–13: 9780615634579

ISBN–10: 0615634575

For every parent who was abused as a child...

Here is hope.

About the Author

Ronae Jull is the HOPE Coach, offering tangible tools for parents gleaned from her own parenting experiences and more than two decades spent coaching families. She holds an undergraduate degree from Walla Walla University, and is currently pursuing a graduate program. Along with her website **Hope Coaching** at ronaejull.com, Ronae is a regular contributor to sites such as YourTango, ParentingExtra, and Shine!Yahoo, and a frequent guest on the live radio program *The Doctor Carol Show* at drcarolshow.com. Ronae's four children are grown, and she enjoys three grandchildren, making global connections through social media, and writing music.

Preface

Child abuse is one of those issues most don't want to think about much. Every few months another dramatic case hits the national news, adding fuel to the idea that, "I guess I didn't really have it that bad", or "That could never happen in *my* family!"

While adults who were abused as children continue living their lives of quiet desperation.

Part of what I do is to reach out to parents of teenagers. Teens have their own set of challenges (to put it mildly), and parents who were confident before often question their sanity when their kids hit adolescence. If those parents were also abused during their own childhood, they are fighting a nearly impossible battle within themselves.

Recently I received the following note.

> *"Parenting teens is hard enough for the best of parents, but when you have been severely abused as children in every way (physically, emotionally, verbally AND sexually) you have no real coping skills for even making it through life, let alone trying to help teens and children through it. Sometimes it seems so extremely hopeless... I am fighting this battle completely alone." ~Anonymous*

This book is dedicated to every parent who experienced abuse as a child.

Acknowledgments

Having my own healing journey means that there were a number of pivotal people that made an enormous impact on my life at different times. This book would never have come to be without each of the following people helping to shape the message.

My older sister, who taught me the rewards of hope, defined personal boundaries, and showed me how to break down the walls of religious isolation and fear.

My last therapist, Dr. James Madia, who believed that total and complete healing was not only possible but was a joy worth pursuing.

My four adult children, who each taught me some of my most powerful lessons, and who remind me often what it really means to practice unconditional love.

My mother. Yes, my mother was one of my abusers. She has now become my greatest cheering section. Among many other gifts from my mother, I gratefully acknowledge her own healing journey that has become such an inspiration to me and many others.

Chapter 1: I Didn't Know I Was Wounded!

Sitting in the driver's seat of an old rickety Chevy station wagon, **Audrey** (all names have been changed) could feel her blood pressure rising. Behind her, three year old Jessica wailed, kicking her feet against the back of Audrey's seat. Suddenly something snapped as Audrey slammed on the brakes. Almost as if she were hearing someone else, she heard her voice yelling over her child's wails, and when that had no effect she raised her hand...

And the cycle continues...

As a single mom, **Lisa** knew she couldn't provide everything for her children that she dreamed of, but she tried hard to give them the best that she could. The only problem she saw was that she got so lonely, and the men she inevitably ended up with certainly weren't the best. After all, who would want to be with a woman "with baggage"?

Sometimes Lisa found herself ignoring the needs of her children to try and meet the needs of her current boyfriend, but they knew they were loved – sure they did! She would always dump the guy when the fighting got bad, convincing herself that she was doing better than her mother who had stayed. But there was always another man... and sometimes they would hurt her children before she could get rid of them.

And the cycle continues...

Jessica watched her daughters growing toward their teenage years with a confusing feeling of dread. The girls' attitudes and challenges of family rules left her feeling overwhelmed and helpless and angry, and many times arguments lasted for days and were never really resolved. Conflict oozed through nearly every interaction, and several times Jessica found herself saying things she regretted. Sometimes she wondered if she would ever get this parenting thing right, since everything she tried seemed to turn out wrong. Then one day her daughter said, "I hate you..."

And the cycle continues...

There is no small definition of abuse that can encompass every way that a child can be wounded by an adult. Audrey, Lisa, Jessica, and millions of other mothers were trying with everything they knew to be the best parent they could be. Yet their parenting left much to be desired. Their parenting hurt their children, sometimes deeply.

There is a key element here that each of these women were not aware of. Handicapped by something completely out of their knowledge and control, each of *these mothers could not be the parent they really wanted to be.*

If you were in a car accident this afternoon – not just a fender bender, but a real serious wreck – what would happen next? You'd be rushed to the hospital where a team of medical professionals would diagnose and treat your injuries with the very best technology and skill available. Then you would embark on the long process of healing, and eventually (at least in our imaginary story) you would be restored to complete health. During your process of healing, it is likely that friends and family would rally around you, doing for you what you could not do for yourself, and supporting you as you regained full use of your physical abilities. While you were walking with crutches, no one would say, *"What's wrong with you – why can't you run up the stairs today?"* You had been wounded – muscles torn and bones broken – and healing would be a time consuming process that no one would criticize you for.

If you're a parent who was abused during your own childhood – physically, emotionally, sexually, or spiritually – you know where this is going.

You were wounded.

Yet, you have been trying to convince yourself that you were not. Or that it was over, done with, in the past, and had nothing to do with the present. That your childhood was *definitely* not going to affect your parenting. After all, it was pretty awful back then, and you were determined to make things better for your own children.

So why do you find yourself raising your voice or your hand (like what happened to you)?

Most moms have a gift for denying their own pain, to the extent that we simply forget their own woundedness. It's a part of that brilliantly creative way of surviving. But when it covers up a problem that has intruded into your present, that denial becomes dysfunction.

When I first sought healing for my own traumatic childhood experiences, I had no idea I was wounded. I thought I had a self-esteem problem. I had a yelling-at-my kids problem (after all, I had strong-willed kids). I believed I was stupid, had a meddling mother, and I couldn't stick with anything I started. And if I could stop feeling depressed and angry, my kids would settle down and listen, and my mother would back off just a bit, maybe life would be better!

My parenting was being controlled by my history, simple as that. In a Twilight Zone-esque type of way, ancient history was reaching out to bite me, and I didn't like it, not one little bit!

If you're a parent who was abused as a child, you are guaranteed to repeat your abuse on some level *unless you do something different.*

So now what?

Chapter 2: Acknowledging the Unthinkable

Taking that first step of acknowledging the unthinkable in your own childhood is one of the most painful things you'll need to do. If you're like most folks, nearly every fiber of your being will be telling you to just forget about it. Yet the fact that your present (parenting) is being controlled by your childhood (the parenting you received) ought to be enough to get your attention.

The first and most powerful step to making a major life change is to acknowledge that a change needs to occur.

Imagine you're standing on one side of a shallow river. There is no bridge or boat you can use to reach the other side, and you don't know how to swim.

The side where you stand is dry and barren, and you've done an amazing job of making it livable. But the other side – that you can barely see in the distance – is lush and green and filled with comfort. There is plenty to eat, warm clothes, and shelter from the hot sun and winter winds. There, too, are familiar faces of those you've known from other places.

It remains a puzzle how you can reach the other side. You want to, but you're afraid. Can't someone just come along and carry you over that rushing water? It looks just a bit frightening, come to think of it, and if you tried to cross you might get swept away by the current.

And yet, the other side sounds like it would be better. Maybe you wouldn't need to always be afraid of doing or saying the wrong thing. Maybe you wouldn't have to use all your energy just to survive, just to figure out how to live, what to do, how to somehow meet your children's needs when you can barely meet your own.

If you want to be free, *if you want to live in control of how you can love your own children*, come with me to the other side. The stepping stones are already in place – only requiring you to take each in its turn.

The first stepping stone that will begin your journey from where you are to where you want to be, is to acknowledge your history.

Own it.

This was done to me.

It wasn't my fault.

Whew! Acknowledging the control that your own childhood has over your parenting today is a painful step on your journey, but an essential one. Most never take this first step. Most never step out onto that first stepping stone having made a decision to find a way to be in control of their parenting.

> *When the pain of staying where you are is greater than the pain of moving forward, you will find a way to move forward.*

Take my hand – let's keep going!

Chapter 3: Seeds of Hope, Time to Begin

I'm the first to admit that simply acknowledging the pain in your own childhood is not going to do much to change your parenting! In fact, for a while it might feel like things are getting worse instead of better. Opening a door to memories that you thought were successfully buried forever can leave you feeling vulnerable and helpless all over again.

Back to your journey of crossing that rushing river on stepping stones. The water is cold, the wind is harsh, and now you're teetering on a wobbly stone out in the middle of the river! If you're anything like every other human being alive, self-preservation will be shouting, *"Go back!"*

Having been on this journey of HOPE let me assure you that the process is worth it. But no assurances by me or someone else will completely relieve your fear, frustration, or even anger.

However, there are a few things that you can do right now to make this part of the journey a little less overwhelming. Take a look at this list, choose what parts to try, and then keep doing what works best for you. After all, you will be carefully nurturing those tiny seeds of HOPE that will enable you to build the life you've only dreamed of!

1. **Keep a HOPE journal**. This is a place to write down what you hope for, so you can remind yourself why you began this journey in the first place. Your why will keep you moving forward even when things are tough. Your HOPE might be your deep desire to give your children the best of who you can be. It might be your need to resolve those old memories rather than locking them up behind deadbolts and barbed wire fences. Whatever your why is, right it down, and keep writing.

2. **Practice a joyful experience**. Now for many of you, this one won't make much sense. Are you kidding? First I ask you to acknowledge old wounds that you thought you were done with forever, and now I ask you to be happy? But it's not as crazy as it sounds at first glance. I'm a firm believer in "acting your way forward" – choosing a better behavior to practice and letting the emotions catch up. After all, if you

wait until you feel better you might be waiting a really long time! It is a revelation to many going through this HOPE process to discover that practicing a joyful experience is not a denial of the pain you are justifiably experiencing. Here's just a few ways to do this: listen to music that makes you feel happy, draw a picture and put it up on the frig, smile at someone on the sidewalk, let someone in ahead of you in line at the grocery store, stand in the sunshine with your eyes closed, wear a bright shirt tomorrow.

3. **Begin paying attention** to others who have gone on this journey before you, and borrow some of their HOPE. Maybe it's just a mental trick, but I assure you that it helps sometimes. When you become overwhelmed with emotion, when your kids are pushing all your buttons and you hear your mother's voice coming out of your mouthwhen you can't find the HOPE you wrote about before and you want to throw up your hands and crawl back to the shore you just stepped out from; when you feel completely and totally alone– borrow some of my HOPE.

4.

Something magical just happened – did you notice?

You just took another step on your journey.

Chapter 4: People Power

Child abuse is an isolating experience by definition. I grew up with siblings, and we never talked about it at the time – we simply survived our 'normal'. Yet in order to create the family you desire, the relationship with your own children that isn't controlled by your own childhood experiences, you'll need people.

But not just *any* people.

Children who grew up with abuse typically react in one of two ways when they become adults – either they trust too much, or not at all.

You either blab your story to anyone who will listen, or have a panic attack just thinking about sharing small bits of it with one person behind closed doors.

But the power of this next step lies in sharing your very heavy burden with another person – **People Power.**

Have you ever played tug-of-war? The power of each side is the cumulative effect of people pulling together; one person pulling alone is easy for the other side to overwhelm.

Your childhood experiences that are controlling your parenting are little dictators pulling you hard in one direction. You need the power of at least one other person to take away some of that pull.

There are many different ways to accomplish this next step. You may choose to share your story with a therapist, someone who is required to keep your confidence. You may have a close friend or confidante that you choose to confide in. If you belong to a religious organization, you may make an appointment with your pastor or priest. Your family physician is another very good option, and someone you can generally trust to hold your secrets gently and with confidentiality. Whoever you choose, here are important guidelines to keep in mind as you move forward.

1. Take time to choose your **People Power** person carefully. With few exceptions, family members are likely not the best choice. Be wise. You are stepping further out into the middle of the river and you're going to need to practice being

careful with your heart. Your significant other is *not* an appropriate person to take this step with. Not that you need to keep your past a secret from them, but your relationship together needs to be focused on other things.

2. Explain to your chosen confidante what you're trying to accomplish. You've acknowledged a painful past experience and need to share it in order not to be controlled by it. Ask if they are willing to simply hear you rather than judging or offering opinions about what you should do or could have done. Breaking isolation's hold over you is a huge step forward, and one that needs to be taken with someone who will gently let *you* be the only one to tell your story.

3. Depending on your experiences, your personality, and your needs of the moment, you can decide to share details or keep this very general. In the tug-of-war between your past and your present, you're putting together evidence that says that your past no longer has control over you.

There is not one person I've talked with who has joyfully embraced the painful process of sharing their abuse history with another person. The sad truth is that those who try to avoid this step inevitably continue repeating those old patterns, and the cycle of abuse continues.

Remember your *why,* and give up your secret's power over you!

There is no getting around this essential step, but there *are* creative ways to make use of People Power. Here are three suggestions that might help.

- The internet has erased complete isolation but added a whole new level of potential dangers. Use the internet as a resource, while practicing safety. Social media is not a safe place to share the burdens you carry from an abusive past, unless it is in a designated group of others who are on the same journey. Instead, use the internet to find someone you can trust with this essential step, then connect by telephone.

- Twelve-Step groups are everywhere. Do a Search for Twelve-Step groups in your area, and get to know the people there. Within these groups there is an expectation of confidentiality, and mentoring is a powerful component of them all.
- If you believe yourself to be totally isolated with no support, you'll need to challenge yourself to step out of your comfort zone if you want to be free from the control of your past. Isolation can become a self-perpetuating habit, but freedom is waiting for you – one stepping stone at a time!

When you have taken this important step in sharing your experiences with another adult, you may feel a whole range of emotions – relief that it's over, frustration that the pain doesn't disappear, deep sadness. Stand still where you are, and remember that many have gone this way before you and have found healing. Never again will you mindlessly repeat the abuse. Now, you need to find a way to move beyond what was, and create the present that is truly *yours.*

Chapter 5: Mirrors and Spotlights

When I was at this point in my own journey, I had what some folks thought was a crazy quirky habit.

I was constantly looking in mirrors.

I would keep the visor down anytime I drove my car, and glance in the mirror often.

Walking down the sidewalk of my small home town, I would glance at the reflection of myself in shop windows.

Every room in my house had a mirror, and I was always looking in them.

Okay you can stop giggling now, although I know it sounds a little weird! But what I was doing was *reminding myself that I was an adult, and of what my daily HOPE CHOICE was.*

Here's how this works.

Those old controlling memories don't go away by magic just because you acknowledge them, begin reminding yourself of your *why*, and break the isolation. They lose their power to control your present by *being replaced* with something new.

Something powerful.

Something that absolutely won't feel 'normal' until you've practiced it for a while.

Something you can only see when you look in a mirror.

Part of the power of **mirrors and spotlights** is that it is impossible to hide!

Mirrors show who you are in the present. Take a moment right now and look in the mirror. Pay attention to how disconnected you feel from who you see. Gather information rather than judging. Stand up straighter and see what that feels like – see what that looks like.

Secrets don't last long when you're looking in a mirror! Practice smiling. Practice throwing your shoulders back and making eye contact with yourself.

Spotlights show what your family is in the present. Take a moment right now and shine a big powerful spotlight on your family. Look closely – it won't be hard to see now that you're not mindlessly following a script written by someone else.

At first, shining a spotlight on your family may show up a whole lot of things that you're going to want to change. In fact it may feel a bit discouraging when you realize how much of what you've been doing has been dictated by your own history. That's what the spotlight is for – to show it up and give you choices.

Look in the mirror.

Shine the spotlight.

Make a HOPE CHOICE.

Remember that this whole journey is about giving you freedom from your abusive past. Taking each step from *where you were* to *where you want to be* builds your foundation of choices. You've acknowledged your history and shared it with another adult. You've made a start at practicing HOPE, and now you're ready to take a close look at WHAT IS, then make some different choices.

Remember back in Chapter 2:

When the pain of staying where you are is greater than the pain of moving forward, you will find a way to move forward.

Using the mirror (literally) and spotlight (in your mind's eye) every single day will help you to keep moving forward.

HOPE CHOICES are just that: a choice that you make to tackle one of those old patterns and find a better way.

Your Spotlight will show all sorts of things, and then you can choose. You might see your habit of yelling at your kids like your mother did, or ignoring them like your father did. You may need to learn more respectful ways to discipline your children, or let go of your need to micro-manage their daily lives. Depending on the ages of your children, learning better ways may seem like a nearly impossible task, but I promise you it is not.

Here are a few things to keep in mind when you begin to practice the mirrors and spotlight step.

1. **Be gentle with yourself**! Just as if you'd been in a car accident, you were wounded. It will take time and practice for your eyes to get used to seeing things more clearly and your heart to learn new and better ways of parenting.
2. Begin with **no more than three** HOPE CHOICES. Write them down in your HOPE Journal. If you get overwhelmed, start with just one.
3. **Enlist the help of your children**!

My daughters were quite young when I 'woke up' and realized that my parenting was perpetuating abuse that I had experienced. I sat down with my girls and explained very briefly that I had made a choice to learn a better way, so that 1) there would be no more corporal punishment, and 2) I would work very hard to stop yelling.

I did great with the first HOPE CHOICE, and lousy with the second.

It took an entire year of practice before we, as a family, became relatively comfortable with the new way. There were many days when I 'lost it' and yelled, being absolutely convinced that my kids would not listen unless I did so. Every single day I would wake up, look in the mirror, shine the spotlight, and remind myself of my HOPE CHOICE. And when I messed up, I'd pick up my courage with both hands and do it again.

Chapter 6: Mine, Yours, and Theirs

Getting to this point in your journey can begin to feel just a little exciting! You're starting to experience what it feels like to actually be able to choose how you interact with your own children rather than mindlessly repeating someone else's attitudes and behaviors. Congratulations!

However, you may also be feeling incredibly frustrated sometimes.

While you've been working very hard to find healing from your abusive history and learn new ways of relating, other members of your family may not share your enthusiasm. One of those human things we all share is that change is uncomfortable, and others in your family may be resisting change with all their might!

Imagine you're slow dancing with a marvelous partner. The lights are right, the mood is familiar, and you can ignore the times he steps on your toes because you've done this so many times you're comfortable with the steps.

Now imagine that suddenly your partner completely changes it up and begins the Jitterbug.

Hold up! This just isn't right! You don't know the moves and try to bow out, but your partner keeps trying to pull you into his dance.

That's what it's like when one family member begins the recovery journey – the rest of the family can feel resentful, and will often do just about anything to get you to go back to the way it was before (even if it was pretty dysfunctional).

Remember, no one likes change very much. You're the only mom (or dad) your kids have known, and kids of any age aren't known for their ability to see the big picture and be patient with uncomfortable change!

This is when it is essential for you to keep a close tab on **what's mine, what's yours, and what's theirs.** Sometimes defining what behaviors and attitudes "belong" to which person is tougher than it seems. Let's take a closer look at all three categories.

What's mine.

You have already 'owned' your own history. You went through abusive experiences while you were growing up that very much shaped the person you became. And now that you've acknowledged your story and shared it, you've begun to practice looking at yourself clearly and shining the spotlight of reality on your parenting relationships.

But be careful! Your spotlight will expose others' behaviors along with your own.

And the only person you can change is yourself.

THAT is one tough concept to internalize, I know. Even as a parent, you can't actually "control" your own children. You can choose family rules and expectations, and enforce consequences if your children choose to ignore them. But the reality is that the only person you can actually *change* is yourself.

Remember in the last chapter my story about letting go of my habit of yelling at my daughters? That behavior on my part was mindlessly straight out of my childhood, copying a habit of my own mother that I despised when I was growing up. However, "mom yelling" was normal for my kids. They had gotten so used to it that they tuned me out. They simply didn't hear me when I spoke softly.

That was the challenge: to keep making my HOPE CHOICE to talk softly even when my children did not respond to it.

Take a look at your HOPE CHOICES, and practice clearly defining what change choices belong to you.

What's yours.

Part of being a parent is the marvelous opportunity to help children learn life lessons as they mature. At whatever moment that you chose to break the cycle of abuse in your family, at that moment, your children now have the chance to grow up free. Free from abuse, from intimidation, from fear. However, it is highly unlikely that they will embrace personal responsibility and accountability, and may in fact vigorously resist any efforts on your part to try to help them behave more respectfully or responsibly.

1. Have brief (age-appropriate) conversations with your children about the habits you have decided to change.
2. Make a list of no more than three things for each child that you can clearly say, "This behavior is YOURS, not mine."
3. Write down the target for change that puts the responsibility for your children's choices on them. Things like, "You will not use curse words around me", "You will put your own clothes in the laundry", or "You will practice getting yourself up on time in the morning." These examples apply to teenagers, but a list is also helpful even with much younger children.
4. Write down appropriate and workable consequences that apply to both of you. For example, if your teenager leaves his dirty laundry in piles on the floor of his room, he may have to put a certain dollar amount in a jar for each article of clothing. If you yell at him about it, *you* could be the one to pay.
5. Especially when old habits are super tough to break between you, decide together on rewards

you can share for a week, a day, or even an hour where each of you are able to own your own 'stuff' and practice the new way.

What's theirs.

Remember that you're breaking the cycle of abuse, letting go of mindlessly repeating old ways, and practicing new patterns of behavior of your choosing. The important word here is **practicing.** That means there is going to be mistakes, restarts, and apologies.

While you're practicing, be ready to shine that spotlight full blast on your family and admit when something is THEIRS.

When you have a horrifying realization that you just repeated a lecture to your teenager that sounded *exactly* like your abusive mother even after all the hard work you've done, **throw it back to 'them'.** While you do need to 'own your own stuff' and apologize when you act out of the old habits, be quick to acknowledge – at least to yourself – where those old habits come from. Depending on the age of your children, sometimes it can be helpful to let your children know where your old habit came from and why it's so important to you that you find a better way.

When this all gets overwhelming or confusing, try this.

Think about your relationship with your child. There will be both big and small things that you'll want to tackle, and even some things that seem just fine. For now, choose **one** behavior pattern that you and your children are struggling with. Start with something simple.

Here's an example taken directly from one of my HOPE Coaching client's experience – with their permission of course. Let's walk through the steps required to help you practice those brand new HOPE CHOICES based on What's Mine, What's Yours, and What's Theirs.

The Problem: *My son leaves piles of dirty laundry on the floor in his room. We argue about it a lot.*

What's Mine: *I nag, I yell, it doesn't work. Then I go clean it up myself.*

What's Yours: *You need to learn to take care of your own laundry.*

What's Theirs: *My internal message comes straight from my mother. I hear that I'm a bad mother if my son is messy or if I don't pick up the slack.*

Your HOPE CHOICE could be: I will no longer nag or yell about the dirty laundry, and I definitely will not clean it up myself.

So now, you can clearly see what behavior belongs to YOU (the only person you can actually change).

Because you're the parent, you have the opportunity to communicate an expectation to your child of being responsible for his own behavior. Remember that he will be most comfortable keeping things the way they always were, so don't expect him to change quickly! And if you set reasonable consequences that you're willing to practice calmly enforcing next time you find dirty laundry in his room, you will begin to transform the relationship between you. Are you beginning to taste the freedom?

Chapter 7: A Grand Adventure

Breaking the cycle of abuse is an amazing experience. If you're smack dab in the middle of it – balancing precariously on one of those wobbly stepping stones in the middle of a rushing river trying to get to the other side – "amazing" is probably not a word you would use to describe it! But think about this:

You get to change the entire course of history!

By following the stepping stones across the river and practicing your HOPE CHOICES, you'll be able to create the life with your family that you always dreamed of but couldn't quite accomplish.

Will it always be easy? Absolutely not. Maybe it never will be what could be called "easy". But there's a big difference between "easy" and "simple".

Human beings are fairly simple at the core. We respond and adapt to our environment, and for the most part we're resilient. The healing that is possible by practicing those simple steps between *where you began* and *where you want to be* have been taken by hundreds and thousands of women and men who made the tough decision **not to have their parenting controlled by their past.**

No matter how mild or severe the abuse that you lived through, there are truly amazing gifts that will result from your healing journey. Someone tried to spoil your life – now look at the goodness that is coming from it!

Let's review your steps to freedom.

1. First, you acknowledge that your parenting was being controlled by your history, not your own choices.
2. Next, you acknowledge what happened, and name it: *This happened to me, and it wasn't my fault!*
3. You break the silence by sharing it with another trusted adult, and grab hold of People Power!
4. By looking in the mirror, you learn to see yourself clearly. And by shining a spotlight on your family, you see your interactions with each member in a new light. This enables you to define your HOPE CHOICES and begin to move into mindful parenting.

5. With each new parenting situation, you practice staying clear on What's Mine, What's Yours, and What's Theirs.
6. You are now poised to create a hope-filled life with your children that is defined by *who you are, not by what someone did to you!*

Now that you've crossed the river, what can you expect on the other side?

Chapter 8: The Path of Least Resistance

Any new skill takes practice to develop, and it's no different with your new way of parenting. Your son didn't learn to skateboard without falling. Your daughter didn't become a budding musician by reading about playing the piano. You won't change your old parenting habits without practice.

Practice: *Choosing a new behavior, making mistakes, trying again, getting better.*

As you move into what I call the Maintenance step of recovery from past trauma, you'll discover that your resistance to your HOPE CHOICES gets less and less over time. You'll sometimes be surprised by the ease with which a new way of relating gets developed, or discouraged when a HOPE CHOICE seems to never quite take hold. Remember, you and your children are human, not perfect robots! No matter how much healing work you do, you (and they) are still a product of your past.

Why not choose the path of least resistance?

The first time you take these step to freedom, it just might feel a little (or a lot) traumatic. You might wonder if you'll ever get through it, if things will ever get better. But as you practice (read the definition of "Practice" above one more time), you'll get better!

So the next time you hear your mother's voice coming out of your mouth, maybe you'll be able to stop your words before they become a torrent. That is truly the path of least resistance, since changing direction in the middle is far easier than starting over at the very beginning.

Look around you. That mother who looks like she's got it all together? It's just as likely that she too was a victim of child abuse, and followed the steps to find healing. That successful businessperson you so admire? He or she may be one of so many who has followed the path to intentionally creating the life with their family that they always dreamed of.

From my own fairly dramatic history of intense abuse, I have found the HOPE and joy of living firmly planted in recovery. It is now my privilege to reach out to others who are lost in their woundedness of history and offer tangible HOPE.

Won't you join me?

Afterword

No list of Resources will be complete. However, I offer the following list as a starting place. I encourage you to do your own careful research and find resources that work to enhance your recovery.

Remember, there is always HOPE!

1. HOPE Coaching with Ronae Jull (ronaejull.com)
2. The American Psychological Association on child sexual abuse
3. American Professional Society on the Abuse of Children
4. The National Child Traumatic Stress Network
5. Child Help USA
6. US National Child Abuse Hotline: 1-800-4-A-CHILD
7. UK NSPCC Childline: 0800-1111
8. Australia Child Abuse Prevention Service: 1800-688-009
9. New Zealand Kidsline: 0800-543-754

10. Visit ChiWorld.org for a list of other international child helplines
11. Joshua Children's Foundation
12. Men Survivors in Transition (UK)
13. Adult Children of Narcissistic Parents (ACONS)
14. DMOZ (Numerous helpful links for adult survivors of abuse)

If you're feeling a bit overwhelmed, that's normal. Take a deep breathe, and begin again. Remember, practice is all about choosing a new way, making mistakes, trying again, and getting better. I've been on this journey for a long time, and I assure you, this healing process will bring you to a place of gentle peace.

.

www.ingramcontent.com/pod-product-compliance
Lightning Source LLC
Chambersburg PA
CBHW071430040426
42445CB00012BA/1330